Ninja Air Fryer Cookbook for Beginners 2024

A Quick Guide to Mastering 80+ Easy, Healthy, Irresistible and Crispy Recipes

Francesca Munro

Table of Contents

Introduction..4

Ninja Air Fryer Max XL 101.......................8

Understanding Your Air Fryer...............12

Practical Tips and Tricks......................23

Cleaning and Maintenance...................30

Breakfast..36

Snacks and Appetizers..........................50

Vegetables and Sides...........................61

Fish and Seafood................................. 72

Poultry Mains.......................................85

Beef, Pork, and Lamb..........................102

Dessert.. 118

Bonus Ninja Air Fryer 1-Week Meal Plan
and Shopping List................................ 133

Measurement Conversions................. 145

Introduction

The Ninja Air Fryer has changed the landscape of cooking by offering a healthier alternative to traditional frying methods. It uses hot air to cook food, requiring significantly less oil than deep frying. This method not only reduces the calorie content of fried foods but also preserves their texture and flavor, making it an ideal choice for health-conscious individuals. The air fryer's ability to deliver crispy, golden results with a fraction of the oil has been a game-changer in the kitchen.

One of the most appealing aspects of the Ninja Air Fryer is its versatility. It's not just a fryer; it's a multi-functional appliance that can bake, roast, and even dehydrate. This versatility opens up a world of culinary possibilities, allowing users to explore a wide range of recipes and cooking methods. From crispy chicken wings to tender roasted vegetables, the Ninja Air Fryer can do it all, making it a must-have appliance in modern kitchens.

The design and user-friendliness of the Ninja Air Fryer are also worth noting. It is intuitively designed, with user-friendly controls and preset functions, making it accessible even to those who are new to cooking. The ease of use encourages experimentation and helps build confidence in the kitchen. Additionally, the Ninja Air Fryer is easy to clean, which is a significant advantage for busy individuals who value convenience and time efficiency.

The Ninja Air Fryer Cookbook for Beginners is more than just a collection of recipes; it is a guide to embracing a healthier lifestyle without sacrificing flavor. The recipes in this cookbook are carefully curated to showcase the versatility of the air fryer, providing a range of options from breakfast to dessert. Each recipe is designed to be easy to follow, with clear instructions and tips for success, making it an ideal companion for those starting their air frying journey.

In addition to the recipes, this cookbook offers valuable insights into the principles of air frying. Understanding how air fryers work, the best practices for achieving the perfect crispiness, and how to adapt traditional recipes for the air fryer are crucial for maximizing the potential of this appliance. This knowledge empowers home cooks to experiment and tailor recipes to their tastes, leading to more enjoyable and successful cooking experiences.

The health benefits of using an air fryer cannot be overstated. By significantly reducing oil usage, air frying offers a healthier way to enjoy fried foods. This cookbook emphasizes recipes that are not only delicious but also nutritious, catering to those looking to maintain a balanced diet. The focus on healthy eating is particularly important in today's fast-paced world, where convenience often trumps nutritional value.

Furthermore, the cookbook includes a section on meal planning and shopping lists, providing a comprehensive approach to meal preparation. This section is particularly useful for beginners, as it takes the guesswork out of cooking and helps in organizing the kitchen and pantry for efficient cooking.

The Ninja Air Fryer Cookbook for Beginners is an essential resource for anyone looking to explore the world of air frying. Whether you're a beginner or an experienced cook, this cookbook offers something for everyone. The recipes, tips, and techniques provided will not only enhance your cooking skills but also inspire you to create healthy, delicious meals for you and your family. Embrace the change, explore new flavors, and enjoy the journey of cooking with the Ninja Air Fryer.

Ninja Air Fryer Max XL 101

At its core, the Ninja® Air Fryer Max XL is a marvel of engineering. It is designed to cater to the needs of modern-day cooking, combining speed, efficiency, and versatility in a compact yet powerful package. This air fryer uses rapid air circulation technology, a method that cooks food by circulating hot air around it. This method not only ensures even cooking but also achieves the much-desired crispy texture that is often associated with traditional frying, but with significantly less oil. The reduction in oil usage is not just a nod to health-conscious cooking; it's a transformation in the way we perceive and enjoy our meals.

The Ninja® Air Fryer Max XL's capacity is a key feature, making it suitable for families. Its ability to cook larger portions means it can cater to a variety of needs, from quick family dinners to hosting friends. This adaptability is essential in today's fast-paced lifestyle, where time and efficiency are of the essence.

Understanding the various functions of the Ninja® Air Fryer Max XL is crucial to unlocking its full potential. Each function is designed to cater to different cooking needs. The air fryer mode is perfect for achieving that crispy, golden texture in foods like french fries or chicken wings. The roast setting allows for tender, well-cooked meats and vegetables, while the bake function can be used for desserts and bread. The reheat function is a convenient feature, ensuring leftovers are warmed through evenly, retaining their flavor and texture.

Another significant aspect of the Ninja® Air Fryer Max XL is its user-friendly interface. The appliance is equipped with intuitive controls and digital displays, making it easy to select cooking modes, adjust temperatures, and set timers. This user-centric design is particularly beneficial for those new to air frying, as it simplifies the cooking process and encourages experimentation with different recipes.

The build quality and design of the Ninja® Air Fryer Max XL also deserve mention. Its sleek, modern aesthetic fits well in any kitchen, while the robust construction ensures durability and longevity. The air fryer basket is designed for easy handling and is dishwasher safe, making cleanup a breeze. This ease of maintenance is a significant advantage, especially for those who use the appliance frequently.

Delving into the culinary possibilities, the Ninja® Air Fryer Max XL offers a realm of exploration. It's not just about frying; it's about reimagining recipes and discovering new ways to prepare your favorite dishes. From crispy vegetables to juicy steaks, and even baked goods, the range of recipes you can create is vast. The air fryer encourages a healthier approach to cooking, allowing for lighter versions of traditionally fried foods without compromising on taste or texture.

The environmental impact of reduced oil usage should not be understated. By using the Ninja® Air Fryer Max XL, not only are you making a healthier choice for yourself, but you're also contributing to a more sustainable cooking practice. Less oil usage means less waste and a smaller carbon footprint, aligning with the growing global consciousness around environmental sustainability.

The Ninja® Air Fryer Max XL is more than an appliance; it's a gateway to a new world of cooking. Its combination of efficiency, versatility, and user-friendliness makes it an indispensable tool in the modern kitchen. Whether you are a novice looking to expand your culinary skills or an experienced chef exploring new cooking methods, the Ninja® Air Fryer Max XL offers a path to delicious, healthier meals prepared with ease and finesse.

Understanding Your Air Fryer

Understanding the Principles of Air Frying

The principle of air frying, a culinary innovation that has redefined healthy cooking, centers around the technique of rapid air circulation. This method, a cornerstone of the Ninja Air Fryer Max XL's functionality, signifies a leap in kitchen technology, merging convenience, health, and flavor in one compact appliance. Understanding this principle is not just about grasping how the machine works; it's about appreciating a new philosophy of cooking.

At the heart of air frying lies the scientific process known as the Maillard reaction. Typically associated with traditional frying, roasting, or baking, this chemical reaction between amino acids and reducing sugars gives browned foods their distinctive flavor. The genius of air frying is its ability to mimic this process with minimal oil, using hot air that circulates rapidly around the food. This method creates a crispy outer layer, achieving a texture and taste comparable to conventional frying.

The Ninja Air Fryer Max XL harnesses this technology effectively. It incorporates a high-powered heating element and a precision-engineered fan that works in tandem to circulate hot air. This hot air surrounds the food placed in the fryer's basket, cooking it evenly and quickly. The appliance's capability to maintain consistent temperature, a critical factor in the Maillard reaction, ensures that each fry, cutlet, or vegetable slice is evenly cooked with a perfect golden-brown finish.

Unlike deep frying, where food is submerged in hot oil, air frying requires significantly less oil. This not only makes air-fried foods healthier but also less burdensome in terms of preparation and cleanup. The reduction of oil is not just beneficial for health; it also alters the flavor profile of foods in a subtle yet distinct manner. Foods retain more of their natural taste and texture, offering a different, often more nuanced, palate experience.

The design of the Ninja Air Fryer Max XL also plays a pivotal role in its cooking efficiency. The fryer's basket, engineered to allow optimal air flow, ensures that every part of the food receives equal heat exposure. This design element is crucial for achieving uniform cooking without having to manually turn or mix the food.

Temperature control is another aspect where the Ninja Air Fryer Max XL shines. The ability to adjust temperatures allows for a range of cooking possibilities, from gently roasting vegetables to crisping up chicken wings. This versatility is key to expanding one's culinary repertoire. It invites experimentation, encouraging users to try air frying for a variety of dishes that wouldn't traditionally be associated with frying.

The timing of cooking in an air fryer is as essential as the temperature. The Ninja Air Fryer Max XL's timer function allows for precise cooking, an essential factor in achieving the desired outcome, whether it's a light crispness or a deep, crunchy texture. This precision in timing and temperature sets air frying apart from conventional methods, where such control can be more challenging to achieve.

Moreover, air frying with the Ninja Air Fryer Max XL presents an environmentally friendlier option. With less oil used, there's less waste and reduced environmental impact. In an age where sustainability is becoming increasingly important, this aspect of air frying is particularly relevant.

Beyond its functional and environmental benefits, air frying with the Ninja Air Fryer Max XL represents a shift towards a more health-conscious cooking style. By significantly reducing the amount of oil, it lowers the calorie content of fried foods and cuts down on unhealthy fats. This is particularly beneficial for those looking to maintain a healthy diet without sacrificing their favorite fried foods.

Learning How Different Ingredients React

Learning how different ingredients react in the Ninja Air Fryer Max XL is an exploration of culinary adaptation and finesse. This journey is not just about substituting one cooking method for another; it's about understanding the unique characteristics of each ingredient and how they interact with the air frying process.

When we consider fatty foods like chicken wings or sausages in the air fryer, we observe that they benefit significantly from this cooking method. As these items cook, the fats naturally render, aiding in the crisping process and adding flavor. This natural oil release means there's no need for additional oil, making the dishes healthier. Moreover, the air fryer circulates hot air around these foods, ensuring they cook evenly and achieve a crispy exterior while retaining moisture inside. This method is excellent for achieving the coveted balance of crunchy and juicy in fried chicken or perfectly browned sausages.

Lean meats, such as chicken breasts or lean pork, present a different scenario. These meats lack the natural fats that aid in crisping, which can lead to dryness if not handled correctly in the air fryer. To counter this, a light brushing of oil or a well-balanced marinade can help. The oil or marinade not only adds moisture but also helps to create a more appealing texture on the surface. It's also crucial to monitor the cooking time closely, as lean meats can easily overcook. The precision of the Ninja Air Fryer Max XL comes into play here, allowing for accurate temperature and time control to achieve the perfect result.

Vegetables in the air fryer transform in delightful ways. While many might not associate air frying with vegetables, it is indeed a fantastic method to cook them. Vegetables like bell peppers, zucchini, and asparagus develop a delightful char and intensified flavors. A light spray of oil and seasoning can elevate their natural flavors, creating dishes that are both healthy and delicious. Root vegetables like potatoes and carrots take on a wonderful crispness, rivaling their traditionally fried counterparts.

Baked goods also adapt beautifully in the air fryer. The circulating hot air makes it akin to a convection oven, ideal for baking small batches of cookies, muffins, or even cakes. The key is to adjust the temperature and cooking time, as the air fryer often cooks faster than a conventional oven. This requires a bit of experimentation, but the results can be surprisingly good, with baked goods emerging evenly cooked and with a pleasing texture.

Seafood in the air fryer is another area where this appliance shines. Delicate items like shrimp or fish fillets cook quickly and can develop a lovely color and texture. Again, a light brush of oil can help in achieving a golden hue, while ensuring the seafood doesn't dry out. The quick cooking time also means that the seafood retains its moisture and tenderness, making the air fryer an excellent tool for healthy, speedy seafood preparations.

In exploring how different ingredients react in the air fryer, the core learning is about balance and understanding. It's about balancing temperatures and cooking times, understanding when to use oil and how much, and getting to know how each ingredient behaves in the hot air stream. This knowledge is not just utilitarian; it's what transforms cooking from a mundane task to an art form. It's what turns the Ninja Air Fryer Max XL from a kitchen appliance into a tool of culinary creativity.

Moreover, this exploration is an ongoing journey. Each ingredient, each dish comes with its own set of variables and nuances. Learning how to adjust and adapt is part of the joy of cooking with the Ninja Air Fryer Max XL. It invites experimentation, encourages adaptation, and rewards with results that are often healthier, faster, and just as delicious as traditional methods.

Adjusting Temperatures and Timings
Adjusting temperatures and timings in the realm of air frying is akin to learning the subtle art of balancing flavors in cooking. The Ninja Air Fryer Max XL offers a diverse range of temperature settings and timing controls, allowing for a precision that can transform the ordinary into the extraordinary. In this chapter, we delve deep into the mastery of these

settings, an essential skill for any air frying enthusiast.

The Role of Temperature in Air Frying

Temperature control is the cornerstone of successful air frying. Each ingredient, with its unique properties, responds differently to heat. High temperatures are perfect for achieving a crispy, golden exterior quickly. This is ideal for foods like French fries or chicken wings, where you want a crunchy texture. The rapid cooking at high heat seals in juices, creating a delicious contrast between the crispy outside and the moist interior.

Lower temperatures, on the other hand, are suited for foods that need thorough cooking without burning or over-crisping. This is particularly relevant for larger or denser foods like a whole chicken or thick vegetable slices. Cooking these items at a lower temperature for a longer period ensures they are cooked through without being charred on the outside.

Understanding the nuances of temperature settings in air frying is not just about following a recipe; it's about adapting to the nature of the food being cooked. It involves recognizing the size, thickness, and texture of the food and adjusting the temperature accordingly. This understanding is what elevates a good dish to a great one in air frying.

Timing: The Unsung Hero of Air Frying

Timing in air frying is just as crucial as temperature. The Ninja Air Fryer Max XL allows for precise timing, a feature that can make a significant difference in the outcome of a dish. Cooking for the right amount of time ensures that food is not under or overdone. For instance, delicate vegetables or thin fish fillets require only a few minutes to cook, whereas denser foods like root vegetables or large cuts of meat need longer.

One common mistake in air frying is underestimating the importance of timing, leading to inconsistent results. Learning to adjust the cooking time based on the quantity and type of food is crucial. This is where the Ninja Air Fryer Max XL's timer becomes an invaluable tool, helping to monitor and adjust cooking times for different dishes.

Preheating: A Critical Step

Preheating the air fryer is a step often overlooked but crucial for optimal cooking. Just as you would preheat a traditional oven, preheating the air fryer ensures that it reaches the desired temperature before the food is introduced. This step is essential for achieving uniform cooking and the desired texture. In the Ninja Air Fryer Max XL, the preheating process is quick and efficient, setting the stage for consistent cooking results.

Preheating also plays a role in reducing cooking time. By starting with a preheated air fryer, the food begins cooking immediately, ensuring a crispier texture, especially on the outside. For recipes that rely on a specific texture or crust, such as breaded items or pastries, preheating can make a significant difference.

Combining Temperature and Timing

The real art in air frying lies in combining the right temperature with the correct timing. This combination is what transforms simple ingredients into delectable dishes. The Ninja Air Fryer Max XL, with its range of settings, offers the flexibility to experiment with this combination, catering to a wide variety of cuisines and preferences.

Learning to adjust these settings based on the dish being prepared is a skill that comes with experience and experimentation. The more one uses the air fryer, the more intuitive these adjustments become. This learning curve is not just about mastering a kitchen appliance; it's about embracing a healthier, more efficient way of cooking.

Practical Tips and Tricks

Navigating the world of air frying with a Ninja Air Fryer Max XL is not just about understanding the basics of the appliance; it's about mastering the small, practical nuances that elevate your cooking. This chapter dedicated to those nuances - the tips and tricks that transform a good air frying experience into a great one.

Ensuring Even Crispiness

One of the keys to perfect air frying is achieving an even, satisfying crispiness. This is not always straightforward, as the nature of air circulation in the fryer can lead to uneven cooking. The solution is simple yet effective - shaking or flipping the items halfway through the cooking process. This technique is especially crucial for smaller items like French fries, chicken nuggets, or vegetables. By manually turning or shaking these items, you ensure that every surface gets equal exposure to the hot air, leading to a uniform texture.

Managing Basket Space

Another critical aspect is managing the space within the air fryer basket. Overcrowding is a common pitfall that can lead to uneven cooking and less than optimal results. The hot air needs to circulate freely around the food for it to cook evenly. When the basket is overcrowded, some pieces get more exposure to the hot air while others get less, resulting in some pieces being overcooked and others undercooked. The trick is to cook in batches if necessary, ensuring there's enough room for the air to move. This might mean a bit more time, but the results are worth it.

Utilizing Accessories

The Ninja Air Fryer Max XL can be enhanced with a range of accessories, each designed to optimize the cooking process for different types of food. For instance, parchment liners can be a great addition, especially when cooking sticky or delicate items. They make cleanup easier and prevent food from sticking to the basket. Grill racks, on the other hand, are perfect for foods that you want to lift off the bottom of the basket, allowing for better air circulation around items like steaks or chops.

Dealing with Smoke and Smell

Sometimes, air frying can produce smoke or strong odors, especially when cooking high-fat foods. To mitigate this, it's advisable to add a little water or a slice of bread at the bottom of the drawer beneath the basket. This helps to catch the fat and reduce smoke. Additionally, regular cleaning of the appliance is crucial in managing smells. Ensuring that the basket and drawer are clean after every use goes a long way in maintaining a fresh, smoke-free cooking environment.

Understanding the Limitations

While the air fryer is a versatile appliance, it's also important to understand its limitations. Not every dish traditionally cooked in an oven or on a stovetop can be replicated in an air fryer. Understanding what works best in your air fryer comes with experience. For instance, batter-fried foods don't fare well as the batter can drip through the basket before it has a chance to set.

Experimentation is Key

Perhaps the most crucial tip is to not be afraid of experimentation. Each air fryer can behave slightly differently, and various foods can react in unexpected ways. The process of discovering the ideal temperature and timing for your favorite dish is a journey in itself. Documenting your experiences, noting down what works and what doesn't, and adjusting your approach accordingly, are all part of the learning curve.

Recipe Adaptations

Adapting traditional recipes for the air fryer is an art that marries the old with the new, blending classic cooking methods with modern technology. The Ninja Air Fryer Max XL, with its advanced features, offers a canvas for such culinary adaptations. This journey of recipe adaptation is not just about tweaking temperatures and timings; it's about reimagining how your favorite dishes can be brought to life in a healthier, yet equally delicious way.

Understanding the Basics of Adaptation

The first step in adapting recipes for the air fryer is understanding how it fundamentally differs from conventional cooking methods. Air frying circulates hot air around the food, requiring less fat than traditional frying. This means that recipes heavy in oil or fat need to be adjusted. For instance, battered foods that are typically deep-fried may need a breadcrumb coating for air frying to achieve a similar crispy texture.

Temperature and Timing Adjustments

One of the key aspects of recipe adaptation is modifying cooking temperatures and times. The air fryer generally cooks food faster than a conventional oven, owing to the concentrated heat and efficient circulation. A rule of thumb is to reduce the cooking temperature by about 25 degrees Fahrenheit compared to the oven recipe, and to shorten the cooking time by 20%. However, this can vary based on the specific dish, so it's important to check the food regularly during the cooking process.

Moisture Management

Another important consideration is moisture. Foods that are naturally moist, like certain vegetables or meats, may not need additional oil. In contrast, drier foods might benefit from a light brushing of oil or a marinade to add moisture and aid in the crisping process. Patting foods dry before cooking is also essential, especially for items like potatoes or chicken, to ensure they crisp up nicely.

Portion Size and Quantity

Adapting recipes also involves considering the size and quantity of the food. Since air fryers cook food by circulating hot air, it's crucial that this air can move freely. Overcrowding the basket can lead to uneven cooking. Foods may need to be cooked in batches, or portions might need to be reduced to fit the size of the air fryer basket.

Adapting Baking Recipes

When it comes to baking, the air fryer can be surprisingly versatile. Baked goods like muffins, small cakes, or cookies can be successfully made in an air fryer. The key here is to monitor the baking closely, as the faster cooking time can lead to overdone edges if not careful. Using baking pans or dishes that fit inside the air fryer basket is crucial, and it's often helpful to lower the cooking temperature to ensure even baking.

Experimentation and Flexibility

Flexibility and a willingness to experiment are vital in the process of recipe adaptation. Not every recipe will translate perfectly on the first try, and some may require a few attempts to get right. Keeping notes on what works and what doesn't can help in refining the process.

In essence, adapting recipes for the Ninja Air Fryer Max XL is an exercise in culinary creativity. It's about respecting the essence of the original recipe while embracing the advantages of air frying. By understanding the principles of air frying and being willing to experiment and adjust, you can transform a wide range of traditional recipes into healthier, air-fried versions that are both delicious and satisfying.

Cleaning and Maintenance

Maintaining and cleaning your Ninja Air Fryer Max XL is a critical aspect of ensuring its longevity and performance. This process, often overlooked in the excitement of cooking, is as essential as the cooking itself. A well-maintained air fryer not only functions better but also ensures that the flavors of your dishes remain pure and uncontaminated by residue from previous cooking sessions.

The Importance of Regular Cleaning

Regular cleaning of your Ninja Air Fryer Max XL is imperative. Each cooking session can leave behind grease, food particles, and residue. Over time, these can build up, potentially affecting the appliance's performance and the taste of your food. More importantly, regular cleaning helps maintain hygiene and food safety standards in your kitchen.

Understanding the Components

The Ninja Air Fryer Max XL comprises several components, each requiring specific cleaning attention. The main parts include the cooking basket, the pan, and the heating element. Familiarizing yourself with these components is the first step towards effective maintenance.

Cleaning the Cooking Basket and Pan

The cooking basket and pan are where the food is directly placed, making them prone to the most residue and grease build-up. Fortunately, these parts are generally dishwasher safe, simplifying the cleaning process. If a dishwasher is not an option, washing them with warm, soapy water is equally effective. It's important to ensure that all food particles are removed, as these can burn and become difficult to clean later. A non-abrasive sponge or brush can be used for scrubbing without damaging the non-stick coating.

Handling the Heating Element

The heating element is a crucial part of the air fryer, responsible for generating the hot air that cooks the food. While it does not often require frequent cleaning, a check-up is necessary to ensure no food particles are stuck to it. Gently wiping the element with a damp cloth can help maintain its efficiency. Caution is advised to avoid any contact with electrical components.

Exterior and Interior Maintenance

The exterior of the Ninja Air Fryer Max XL, while not directly involved in the cooking process, should also be kept clean. A simple wipe with a damp cloth is usually sufficient. The interior, however, might need a more thorough cleaning, especially if any food particles have escaped the basket. A damp cloth or sponge can be used to clean the interior after the appliance has cooled down.

Post-Cleaning Checks

After cleaning, it's important to reassemble all parts correctly. Incorrect assembly can lead to inefficient cooking and potential damage to the appliance. Ensuring that the basket and pan are properly seated and that no residual water is left in the machine will keep your air fryer in optimal condition.

Periodic Deep Cleaning

In addition to regular cleaning after use, periodic deep cleaning is advisable. This involves a more thorough cleaning of all components and can help in removing any grease or residue build-up that regular cleaning might miss. This process, done every few months, depending on usage, ensures that your air fryer remains in top condition.

Avoiding Common Cleaning Mistakes

Common cleaning mistakes include using abrasive materials, which can scratch and damage the non-stick surface, and immersing the main unit in water, which can damage the electrical components. Understanding what cleaning materials and methods are safe for your air fryer is crucial in maintaining its longevity.

Regular and thorough cleaning of your Ninja Air Fryer Max XL is not just about cleanliness; it's about preserving its functionality and ensuring the quality of your cooking. This maintenance regime is a testament to the respect and care you have for your kitchen appliances, reflecting the pride you take in your culinary creations. By the end of this chapter, armed with the knowledge of proper cleaning and maintenance, you will be well on your way to becoming an air frying enthusiast, capable of creating delicious, healthier dishes while ensuring your appliance lasts for years to come.

Breakfast

• Air Fryer Breakfast Burritos:

Ingredients:
• 6 large eggs

• 1 cup diced bell peppers and onions

• 1 cup cooked sausage, crumbled

• 1 cup shredded cheese

• 4 large tortillas

Instructions:
• In a bowl, scramble eggs and mix in diced vegetables and cooked sausage.

• Spoon the egg mixture onto each tortilla, sprinkle with shredded cheese, and fold into burritos.

• Preheat the air fryer to 375°F (190°C).

• Place burritos in the air fryer basket seam side down.

• Air fry for 8-10 minutes until the burritos are crispy and golden.

• Serve hot, optionally with salsa or sour cream.

Servings: 4 *Calories:* 420 per serving *Prep Time:* 15 minutes

Blueberry Pancake Bites:

Ingredients:
• 2 cups pancake batter

• 1 cup fresh blueberries

Instructions:
• Fill small molds with pancake batter.

• Drop fresh blueberries into each mold.

• Preheat the air fryer to 350°F (180°C).

• Place the molds in the air fryer basket.

• Air fry for 5-7 minutes until the pancake bites are golden and cooked through.

• Serve as a delightful breakfast treat.

Servings: 6 *Calories:* 180 per serving *Prep Time:* 10 minutes

Avocado and Egg Toast:

Ingredients:
• 4 slices of whole-grain bread

• 2 ripe avocados

• 4 large eggs

Instructions:
• Toast the bread slices until golden.

• Mash avocados and spread evenly on toasted bread.

• Fry eggs to desired doneness.

• Place a fried egg on each slice of avocado toast.

• Preheat the air fryer to 375°F (190°C).

• Air fry for 3-5 minutes until the edges of the bread are crispy.

Servings: 4 *Calories:* 280 per serving *Prep Time:* 15 minutes

Feel free to adjust servings and ingredients based on your preferences!

Banana Walnut Muffins:

Ingredients:
• 2 cups banana muffin batter

• 1/2 cup chopped walnuts

Instructions:
• Fill muffin cups with banana batter.

• Sprinkle chopped walnuts on top.

• Preheat the air fryer to 350°F (180°C).

• Place muffin cups in the air fryer basket.

• Air fry for 12-15 minutes until muffins are cooked through.

• Allow to cool before serving.

Servings: 12 *Calories:* 180 per serving *Prep Time:* 20 minutes

French Toast Sticks:

Ingredients:
• 8 slices of bread

• 2 large eggs

• 1/2 cup milk

• 1 teaspoon cinnamon

• Maple syrup for serving

Instructions:
• Cut bread slices into sticks.

• In a bowl, whisk together eggs, milk, and cinnamon.

• Dip bread sticks in the egg mixture.

• Preheat the air fryer to 375°F (190°C).

• Place the sticks in the air fryer basket.

• Air fry for 6-8 minutes until golden.

• Serve with maple syrup.

Servings: 4 *Calories:* 220 per serving *Prep Time:* 15 minutes

Sausage and Egg Breakfast Sandwich:

Ingredients:
• 4 English muffins, split and toasted

• 4 sausage patties

• 4 large eggs

• 4 slices of cheese

Instructions:
• Cook sausage patties in the air fryer until browned.

• Fry eggs to desired doneness.

• Assemble sandwiches with muffins, sausage, egg, and cheese.

• Preheat the air fryer to 350°F (180°C).

• Place sandwiches in the air fryer basket.

• Air fry for 3-5 minutes until the cheese is melted.

• Serve hot.

Servings: 4 *Calories:* 380 per serving *Prep Time:* 20 minutes

Spinach and Feta Omelette:

Ingredients:
• 4 eggs

• 1 cup fresh spinach, chopped

• 1/2 cup feta cheese, crumbled

Instructions:
• Whisk eggs in a bowl.

• Add chopped spinach and crumbled feta, mix well.

• Preheat the air fryer to 350°F (180°C).

• Pour the egg mixture into the air fryer basket.

• Air fry for 8-10 minutes until the omelette is set.

• Fold and serve hot.

Servings: 2 *Calories:* 220 per serving *Prep Time:* 10 minutes

Cinnamon Sugar Donuts:

Ingredients:
• 1 can biscuit dough

• 1/2 cup cinnamon sugar

Instructions:

• Cut biscuit dough into rounds.

• Preheat the air fryer to 375°F (190°C).

• Place dough rounds in the air fryer basket.

• Air fry for 5-7 minutes until golden.

• Coat with cinnamon sugar while warm.

• Enjoy these delightful donuts.

Servings: 8 *Calories:* 150 per serving *Prep Time:* 15 minutes

Breakfast Pizza:

Ingredients:

• 1 pizza dough

• 4 eggs

• 6 slices bacon, cooked and crumbled

• 1 cup shredded cheese

Instructions:
• Roll out pizza dough on a flat surface.

• Top with eggs, bacon, and shredded cheese.

• Preheat the air fryer to 375°F (190°C).

• Transfer the pizza to the air fryer basket.

• Air fry for 10-12 minutes until the crust is golden.

• Slice and savor your breakfast pizza.

Servings: 4 *Calories:* 280 per serving *Prep Time:* 25 minutes

Fruit Parfait:

Ingredients:
• 2 cups Greek yogurt

• 1 cup granola

• 1 cup mixed fruits (berries, banana slices)

Instructions:
• Layer Greek yogurt, granola, and mixed fruits in jars.

• Preheat the air fryer to 325°F (160°C).

• Place jars in the air fryer basket.

• Air fry for 5 minutes for a warm parfait.

• Enjoy this delightful and healthy breakfast.

Servings: 2 *Calories:* 280 per serving *Prep Time:* 15 minutes

Feel free to indulge in these delicious breakfast options!

Blueberry Breakfast Cobbler:

Ingredients:
• 2 cups blueberries

• 1 cup oats

• 1/2 cup almond flour

• 1/4 cup maple syrup

• 2 tbsp coconut oil

Instructions:
• Mix blueberries with maple syrup, place in an air fryer-safe dish.

• In a bowl, combine oats, almond flour, and melted coconut oil.

• Spread oat mixture over blueberries.

• Air fry at 375°F (190°C) for 15-18 minutes until golden.

Servings: 4 *Calories:* 220 per serving *Prep Time:* 10 minutes

Granola:

Ingredients:

• 3 cups rolled oats

• 1 cup mixed nuts

• 1/4 cup honey

• 2 tbsp coconut oil

• 1 tsp vanilla extract

Instructions:
• Mix oats, mixed nuts, honey, melted coconut oil, and vanilla.

• Spread on the air fryer tray.

• Air fry at 300°F (150°C) for 15-20 minutes, stirring halfway.

Servings: 8 *Calories:* 180 per serving *Prep Time:* 10 minutes

Mixed Berry Muffins:

Ingredients:
• 2 cups mixed berries

• 2 cups flour

• 1 cup sugar

• 1/2 cup melted butter

• 1 cup milk

Instructions:

- Combine flour, sugar, melted butter, and milk.

- Fold in mixed berries.

- Spoon batter into muffin cups.

- Air fry at 350°F (180°C) for 15-18 minutes until golden.

Servings: 12 *Calories:* 180 per serving *Prep Time:* 15 minutes

Snacks and Appetizers

Air-Fried Spring Rolls:

Ingredients:
• 1 cup shredded cabbage

• 1 cup julienned carrots

• 1 cup cooked and shredded chicken

• Spring roll wrappers

• Soy sauce for dipping

Instructions:
• Mix cabbage, carrots, and shredded chicken.

• Place a spoonful of the mixture in a spring roll wrapper.

• Roll tightly, sealing edges with water.

• Air fry at 375°F (190°C) for 10-12 minutes until crispy.

Servings: 4 *Calories:* 150 per serving *Prep Time:* 20 minutes

Classic French Fries:

Ingredients:

• 4 large potatoes, cut into fries

• 2 tbsp olive oil

• Salt and pepper to taste

• Ketchup for dipping

Instructions:

• Toss potato fries with olive oil, salt, and pepper.

• Air fry at 375°F (190°C) for 18-20 minutes until golden.

• Serve with ketchup.

Servings: 4 Calories: 180 per serving *Prep Time:* 15 minutes

Apple Chips:

Ingredients:

• 4 apples, thinly sliced

• 1 tsp cinnamon

• 1 tbsp sugar

Instructions:

• Toss apple slices with cinnamon and sugar.

• Arrange in a single layer in the air fryer.

• Air fry at 350°F (180°C) for 10-12 minutes until crispy.

Servings: 4 Calories: 80 per serving *Prep Time:* 10 minutes

Easy Garlic-Parmesan French Fries:

Ingredients:

• 4 large potatoes, cut into fries

• 2 tbsp olive oil

• 2 cloves garlic, minced

• 1/4 cup grated Parmesan

• Salt to taste

Instructions:

• Toss potato fries with olive oil and garlic.

• Air fry at 375°F (190°C) for 18-20 minutes until golden.

• Sprinkle with Parmesan and salt.

Servings: 4 *Calories:* 200 per serving *Prep Time:* 15 minutes

Onion Rings:

Ingredients:

• 2 large onions, sliced into rings

• 1 cup all-purpose flour

• 1 tsp paprika

• 1/2 tsp garlic powder

• 1 cup buttermilk

• 1 cup breadcrumbs

• Salt and pepper to taste

• Cooking spray

Instructions:

• Mix flour, paprika, and garlic powder.

• Dip onion rings in buttermilk, then coat in flour mixture.

• Dip in buttermilk again, then coat in breadcrumbs.

• Air fry at 375°F (190°C) for 10-12 minutes until golden.

Servings: 4 *Calories:* 180 per serving *Prep Time:* 20 minutes

Crunchy Pork Egg Rolls:

Ingredients:

• 1 lb ground pork

• 1 cup shredded cabbage

• 1/2 cup shredded carrots

• 2 cloves garlic, minced

• 1 tbsp soy sauce

• Egg roll wrappers

Instructions:

• Cook pork, cabbage, carrots, and garlic.

• Add soy sauce, spoon mixture onto egg roll wrappers.

• Roll tightly, air fry at 375°F (190°C) for 12-15 minutes until crispy.

Servings: 4 *Calories:* 220 per serving *Prep Time:* 25 minutes

Mushroom and Gruyère Tarts:

Ingredients:

• Puff pastry sheets

• 1 cup sliced mushrooms

• 1 cup shredded Gruyère cheese

• 1 tbsp olive oil

• Salt and pepper to taste

Instructions:

• Cut puff pastry into squares.

• Mix mushrooms, Gruyère, olive oil, salt, and pepper.

• Top pastry with mixture, air fry at 375°F (190°C) for 10-12 minutes until golden.

Servings: 4 *Calories:* 250 per serving *Prep Time:* 15 minutes

Panko-Breaded Mozzarella Sticks:

Ingredients:

• Mozzarella sticks

• 1 cup panko breadcrumbs

• 1/2 cup flour

• 2 eggs, beaten

• Marinara sauce for dipping

Instructions:

• Coat mozzarella sticks in flour, dip in eggs, then coat in panko.

• Air fry at 375°F (190°C) for 6-8 minutes until golden.

• Serve with marinara.

Servings: 4 *Calories:* 160 per serving *Prep Time:* 15 minutes

Scotch Eggs:

Ingredients:

• 4 hard-boiled eggs

• Sausage meat

• 1 cup breadcrumbs

• 2 eggs, beaten

• Cooking oil

Instructions:

• Wrap hard-boiled eggs in sausage meat.

• Dip in beaten eggs, coat in breadcrumbs.

• Air fry at 375°F (190°C) for 15-18 minutes until sausage is cooked.

Servings: 4 Calories: 280 per serving *Prep Time:* 30 minutes

Stuffed Jalapeño Poppers:

Ingredients:

• Jalapeño peppers

• Cream cheese

• Shredded cheddar

• Bacon strips

Instructions:

• Cut jalapeños, fill with cream cheese and cheddar.

• Wrap with bacon, secure with toothpicks.

• Air fry at 375°F (190°C) for 10-12 minutes until bacon is crispy.

Servings: 4 *Calories:* 200 per serving *Prep Time:* 20 minutes

Vegetables and Sides

Roasted Shishito Peppers with Lime:

Ingredients:
• 1 lb shishito peppers

• Olive oil

• Salt

• Lime wedges for serving

Instructions:
• Toss peppers with olive oil and salt.

• Air fry at 375°F (190°C) for 8-10 minutes until blistered.

• Serve with lime wedges.

Servings: 4 *Calories:* 40 per serving *Prep Time:* 10 minutes

Breaded Artichoke Hearts:

Ingredients:

• Canned artichoke hearts

• Flour

• Eggs

• Breadcrumbs

• Marinara sauce for dipping

Instructions:

• Dip artichoke hearts in flour, eggs, then breadcrumbs.

• Air fry at 375°F (190°C) for 10-12 minutes until golden.

• Serve with marinara.

Servings: 4 *Calories:* 120 per serving *Prep Time:* 15 minutes

Crispy Broccoli:

Ingredients:

• Fresh broccoli florets

• Olive oil

• Garlic powder

• Parmesan cheese (optional)

Instructions:

• Toss broccoli with olive oil and garlic powder.

• Air fry at 375°F (190°C) for 12-15 minutes until crispy.

• Optional: sprinkle with Parmesan.

Servings: 4 *Calories:* 50 per serving *Prep Time:* 10 minutes

Buffalo Cauliflower:

Ingredients:

• Cauliflower florets

• Buffalo sauce

• Butter

• Ranch dressing for dipping

Instructions:

• Mix cauliflower with melted butter and buffalo sauce.

• Air fry at 375°F (190°C) for 15-18 minutes until crispy.

• Serve with ranch.

Servings: 4 *Calories:* 80 per serving *Prep Time:* 15 minutes

Nacho Kale Chips:

Ingredients:

- Kale leaves, destemmed

- Olive oil

- Nacho seasoning

Instructions:

- Massage kale with olive oil and nacho seasoning.

- Air fry at 375°F (190°C) for 8-10 minutes until crispy.

Servings: 4 *Calories:* 30 per serving *Prep Time:* 10 minutes

Fried Brussels Sprouts with Honey-Sriracha Sauce:

Ingredients:

- Brussels sprouts, halved

- Olive oil

• Honey-Sriracha sauce

Instructions:

• Toss sprouts with olive oil.

• Air fry at 375°F (190°C) for 12-15 minutes until golden.

• Drizzle with honey-Sriracha sauce.

Servings: 4 Calories: 60 per serving Prep Time: 15 minutes

Savory Roasted Sweet Potatoes:

Ingredients:

• 2 large sweet potatoes, peeled and diced

• Olive oil

• Salt and pepper

• Dried rosemary (optional)

Instructions:

• Toss sweet potatoes with olive oil, salt, and pepper.

• Air fry at 400°F (200°C) for 20-25 minutes until tender.

• Optional: sprinkle with dried rosemary.

Servings: 4 *Calories:* 120 per serving *Prep Time:* 10 minutes

Roasted Corn on the Cob:

Ingredients:

• 4 ears of corn, husked

• Butter

• Salt

Instructions:

• Rub corn with butter and sprinkle with salt.

• Air fry at 375°F (190°C) for 15-18 minutes, turning halfway.

Servings: 4 *Calories:* 80 per serving *Prep Time:* 5 minutes

Glazed Carrots and Sweet Potatoes:

Ingredients:

• 1 cup baby carrots

• 1 large sweet potato, sliced

• Olive oil

• Honey

• Cinnamon

Instructions:

• Toss carrots and sweet potatoes with olive oil, honey, and cinnamon.

• Air fry at 375°F (190°C) for 15-18 minutes until glazed.

Servings: 4 *Calories:* 100 per serving *Prep Time:* 10 minutes

Fried Green Tomatoes:

Ingredients:

• 4 green tomatoes, sliced

• Flour

• Eggs

• Cornmeal

• Salt and pepper

Instructions:

• Dip tomato slices in flour, eggs, then cornmeal.

• Air fry at 375°F (190°C) for 10-12 minutes until crispy.

Servings: 4 Calories: 90 per serving *Prep Time:* 15 minutes

Eggplant Parmesan:

Ingredients:

• 1 large eggplant, sliced

• Marinara sauce

• Mozzarella cheese

• Parmesan cheese

• Bread crumbs

Instructions:

• Coat eggplant slices in breadcrumbs, air fry until golden.

• Layer in a baking dish with marinara and cheeses.

• Air fry at 375°F (190°C) for 12-15 minutes until bubbly.

Servings: 4 *Calories:* 150 per serving *Prep Time:* 20 minutes

These flavorful dishes are beginner-friendly, allowing you to explore the world of air-frying with ease. Enjoy the delightful tastes of these roasted and fried delights!

Fish and Seafood

Salmon on a Bed of Fennel and Carrot

Ingredients:
• 2 salmon fillets

• 1 fennel bulb, thinly sliced

• 2 carrots, julienned

• Olive oil, salt, and pepper to taste

Instructions:
• Preheat the air fryer to 375°F (190°C).

• Season salmon fillets with salt and pepper.

• Toss fennel and carrot with olive oil, salt, and pepper.

• Place salmon on a bed of fennel and carrot in the air fryer basket.

• Air fry for 10-12 minutes or until salmon is cooked through.

Servings: 2
Calories: Approximately 350 per serving
Prep Time: 15 minutes

Louisiana Fried Catfish

Ingredients:

• 2 catfish fillets

• 1 cup cornmeal

• 1 tablespoon Cajun seasoning

• Cooking spray

Instructions:

• In a bowl, mix cornmeal and Cajun seasoning.

• Coat catfish fillets in the cornmeal mixture.

• Preheat air fryer to 400°F (200°C).

• Place catfish in the air fryer basket, spray with cooking spray.

• Air fry for 12-15 minutes or until golden brown.

Servings: 2
Calories: Approximately 300 per serving
Prep Time: 10 minutes

Lemongrass Steamed Tuna

Ingredients:
• 2 tuna steaks

• 2 lemongrass stalks, chopped

• 2 cloves garlic, minced

• Soy sauce and sesame oil to taste

Instructions:
• Mix chopped lemongrass, minced garlic, soy sauce, and sesame oil.

• Marinate tuna steaks in the mixture for 15 minutes.

• Preheat air fryer to 375°F (190°C).

• Place tuna in the air fryer basket.

• Air fry for 8-10 minutes or until tuna is cooked to your liking.

Servings: 2
Calories: Approximately 250 per serving
Prep Time: 25 minutes (including marination)

Beer-Battered Fish and Chips

Ingredients:

• 2 white fish fillets

• 1 cup all-purpose flour

• 1 cup beer

• Salt and pepper to taste

• Potatoes, cut into fries

Instructions:

• In a bowl, whisk flour, beer, salt, and pepper into a batter.

• Dip fish fillets in the batter.

• Preheat air fryer to 400°F (200°C).

• Place battered fish and fries in the air fryer basket.

• Air fry for 15-20 minutes or until golden brown.

Servings: 2
Calories: Approximately 400 per serving
Prep Time: 30 minutes

Classic Fish Sandwiches with Quick Tartar Sauce

Ingredients:

- 2 white fish fillets

- 1 cup breadcrumbs

- 1 egg

- Salt and pepper to taste

- Burger buns

- Lettuce, tomato, and pickles for topping

Quick Tartar Sauce:

- 1/2 cup mayonnaise

- 2 tablespoons pickles, finely chopped

- 1 tablespoon Dijon mustard

- 1 tablespoon fresh lemon juice

Instructions:

• Dip fish fillets in beaten egg, coat with breadcrumbs.

• Preheat air fryer to 375°F (190°C).

• Air fry fish for 12-15 minutes until golden and cooked.

• Mix tartar sauce ingredients, spread on buns, add fish, lettuce, tomato, and pickles.

Servings: 2
Calories: Approximately 450 per serving
Prep Time: 25 minutes

Crunchy Baja Fish Tacos with Mango Salsa

Ingredients:

• 2 white fish fillets

• 1 cup cornmeal

• Taco shells

- Shredded cabbage

- Mango salsa (mango, red onion, cilantro, lime juice)

Instructions:

- Coat fish in cornmeal, preheat air fryer to 375°F (190°C).

- Air fry fish for 10-12 minutes until crispy.

- Fill taco shells with shredded cabbage, top with fish, and mango salsa.

Servings: 2
Calories: Approximately 380 per serving
Prep Time: 30 minutes

Cilantro-Lime Fried Shrimp

Ingredients:
- 1 pound shrimp, peeled and deveined

- 1 cup flour

- 1 cup breadcrumbs

- 2 eggs

- Zest of 1 lime

- Fresh cilantro, chopped

- Salt and pepper to taste

- Lime wedges for serving

Instructions:

- Dredge shrimp in flour, dip in beaten eggs, coat with breadcrumbs mixed with lime zest and cilantro.

- Preheat air fryer to 400°F (200°C).

- Air fry shrimp for 8-10 minutes until golden, serve with lime wedges.

Servings: 4
Calories: Approximately 300 per serving

Prep Time: 20 minutes

Island Coconut Shrimp with Pineapple Sauce

Ingredients:

• 1 pound large shrimp, peeled and deveined

• 1 cup shredded coconut

• 1 cup panko breadcrumbs

• 2 eggs

• Pineapple sauce (pineapple, soy sauce, ginger)

Instructions:

• Dip shrimp in beaten eggs, coat with a mixture of shredded coconut and panko breadcrumbs.

• Preheat air fryer to 375°F (190°C).

• Air fry shrimp for 12-15 minutes until coconut is golden, serve with pineapple sauce.

Servings: 4
Calories: Approximately 320 per serving
Prep Time: 25 minutes

Scallops and Spring Veggies

Ingredients:

• 1 pound sea scallops

• 2 cups spring vegetables (asparagus, peas, baby carrots)

• Olive oil

• Lemon juice

• Salt and pepper to taste

Instructions:

• Season scallops with salt, pepper, and a drizzle of olive oil.

• Toss spring veggies with olive oil, salt, and pepper.

• Preheat air fryer to 400°F (200°C).

• Air fry scallops for 6-8 minutes, tossing veggies halfway, until scallops are golden.

Servings: 4
Calories: Approximately 250 per serving
Prep Time: 20 minutes

Crab Cakes

Ingredients:
• 1 pound lump crabmeat

• 1/2 cup breadcrumbs

• 1/4 cup mayonnaise

• 1 egg

• Dijon mustard, Old Bay seasoning

• Lemon wedges

Instructions:

• Mix crabmeat, breadcrumbs, mayonnaise, egg, Dijon mustard, and Old Bay seasoning.

• Form into patties and chill.

• Preheat air fryer to 375°F (190°C).

• Air fry crab cakes for 12-15 minutes until golden, serve with lemon wedges.

Servings: 4
Calories: Approximately 280 per serving
Prep Time: 30 minutes

Poultry Mains

Chicken Fajitas

Ingredients:
• 1 pound chicken breast, sliced

• Bell peppers, sliced

• Onion, sliced

• Fajita seasoning

• Flour tortillas

Instructions:
• Toss chicken, peppers, and onion with fajita seasoning.

• Preheat air fryer to 400°F (200°C).

• Air fry for 15-18 minutes, stirring halfway.

• Serve in warm tortillas.

Servings: 4
Calories: Approximately 350 per serving
Prep Time: 25 minutes

Warm Chicken and Spinach Salad

Ingredients:
• 1 pound chicken thighs, cooked and shredded

• Fresh spinach

• Cherry tomatoes, halved

• Balsamic vinaigrette

Instructions:
• Season chicken with salt and pepper, air fry until cooked.

• Combine spinach, cherry tomatoes, and chicken.

• Drizzle with balsamic vinaigrette.

Servings: 2

Calories: Approximately 280 per serving
Prep Time: 20 minutes

Spicy Chicken Meatballs

Ingredients:
• 1 pound ground chicken

• Bread crumbs, egg

• Chili powder, cayenne

• BBQ sauce for dipping

Instructions:
• Mix ground chicken, bread crumbs, egg, chili powder, and cayenne.

• Form into meatballs.

• Air fry at 375°F (190°C) for 15-20 minutes.

• Serve with BBQ sauce.

Servings: 4
Calories: Approximately 240 per serving

Prep Time: 30 minutes

Italian Chicken Parmesan

Ingredients:
• Chicken breasts

• Marinara sauce, mozzarella, Parmesan

• Bread crumbs, egg

• Spaghetti

Instructions:
• Coat chicken in egg and breadcrumbs, air fry until crispy.

• Top with marinara and cheese, air fry until cheese melts.

• Serve over cooked spaghetti.

Servings: 4
Calories: Approximately 420 per serving
Prep Time: 40 minutes

Easy General Tso's Chicken

Ingredients:

• 1 pound chicken thighs, diced

• 1/4 cup soy sauce

• 2 tablespoons hoisin sauce

• 1 tablespoon rice vinegar

• 2 tablespoons brown sugar

• 2 cloves garlic, minced

• 1 teaspoon ginger, grated

• 2 tablespoons cornstarch

• Green onions and sesame seeds for garnish

Instructions:

• In a bowl, mix soy sauce, hoisin sauce, rice vinegar, brown sugar, garlic, and ginger.

• Toss diced chicken in cornstarch until coated.

• Air fry chicken until crispy.

• Toss crispy chicken in the sauce mixture.

• Garnish with chopped green onions and sesame seeds.

Servings: 4
Calories: Approximately 380 per serving
Prep Time: 35 minutes

Spicy Coconut Chicken Wings

Ingredients:

• 1.5 pounds chicken wings

• 1/2 cup coconut milk

• 2 tablespoons lime juice

- 2 tablespoons Sriracha

- 1 teaspoon garlic powder

- Cilantro and shredded coconut for garnish

Instructions:

- Marinate wings in coconut milk, lime juice, Sriracha, and garlic powder.

- Air fry wings until crispy.

- Garnish with chopped cilantro and shredded coconut.

Servings: 4
Calories: Approximately 320 per serving
Prep Time: 40 minutes

Chili Ranch Chicken Wings

Ingredients:

- 1.5 pounds chicken wings

- 2 tablespoons ranch seasoning

- 1 tablespoon chili powder

- 2 tablespoons olive oil

- Ranch dressing for dipping

Instructions:

- Toss wings in olive oil, ranch seasoning, and chili powder.

- Air fry wings until golden.

- Serve with ranch dressing for dipping.

Servings: 4
Calories: Approximately 300 per serving
Prep Time: 35 minutes

Crispy Chicken Thighs with Roasted Carrots

Ingredients:

- 1.5 pounds chicken thighs

- 1 pound carrots, peeled and sliced

- 2 tablespoons olive oil

- 1 teaspoon paprika

- 1 teaspoon garlic powder

- 1 teaspoon thyme

Instructions:

- Season chicken thighs with paprika, garlic powder, and thyme.

- Air fry chicken and carrots until crispy and tender.

Servings: 4
Calories: Approximately 400 per serving
Prep Time: 30 minutes

Buffalo Chicken Strips

Ingredients:

• 1.5 pounds chicken breast, cut into strips

• 1/2 cup buffalo sauce

• 1/4 cup melted butter

• 1 teaspoon garlic powder

• 1 teaspoon onion powder

Instructions:

• Dip chicken strips in melted butter and buffalo sauce.

• Air fry strips until cooked.

• Sprinkle with garlic and onion powder.

Servings: 4
Calories: Approximately 340 per serving
Prep Time: 25 minutes

Chicken Satay

Ingredients:

• 1.5 pounds chicken breast, sliced

• 1/4 cup soy sauce

• 2 tablespoons peanut butter

• 1 tablespoon honey

• 1 teaspoon curry powder

• Skewers for grilling

Instructions:

• Mix soy sauce, peanut butter, honey, and curry powder for marinade.

• Thread chicken slices onto skewers, coat with marinade.

• Air fry at 375°F for 15-20 minutes, turning halfway.

Servings: 4
Calories: Approximately 280 per serving
Prep Time: 30 minutes

Crispy Chicken Tenders

Ingredients:
- 1.5 pounds chicken tenders

- 1 cup buttermilk

- 1 cup breadcrumbs

- 1 teaspoon paprika

- 1 teaspoon garlic powder

- Cooking spray

Instructions:

- Soak chicken tenders in buttermilk.

- Coat tenders with breadcrumbs, paprika, and garlic powder.

• Air fry at 400°F for 12-15 minutes, flipping halfway.

Servings: 4
Calories: Approximately 320 per serving
Prep Time: 25 minutes

Chicken Cordon Bleu

Ingredients:
• 1.5 pounds chicken breasts

• 4 slices ham

• 4 slices Swiss cheese

• 1 cup breadcrumbs

• 2 eggs, beaten

Instructions:

• Flatten chicken breasts, add ham and cheese, roll.

• Dip rolls in beaten eggs, coat with breadcrumbs.

• Air fry at 375°F for 20-25 minutes.

Servings: 4
Calories: Approximately 380 per serving
Prep Time: 35 minutes

Spicy Air-Crisped Chicken and Potatoes

Ingredients:

• 1.5 pounds chicken thighs

• 1.5 pounds baby potatoes

• 2 tablespoons olive oil

• 1 teaspoon smoked paprika

• 1 teaspoon cayenne pepper

Instructions:

• Toss chicken and potatoes in olive oil, paprika, and cayenne.

• Air fry at 390°F for 25-30 minutes, shaking occasionally.

Servings: 4
Calories: Approximately 420 per serving
Prep Time: 40 minutes

Buttermilk Fried Chicken

Ingredients:

• 1.5 pounds chicken pieces

• 2 cups buttermilk

• 2 cups flour

• 1 teaspoon paprika

• 1 teaspoon garlic powder

Instructions:

• Soak chicken in buttermilk.

• Coat chicken with flour, paprika, and garlic powder.

• Air fry at 375°F for 30-35 minutes.

Servings: 4
Calories: Approximately 400 per serving
Prep Time: 45 minutes

Korean Chicken Wings

Ingredients:

• 1.5 pounds chicken wings

• 1/4 cup soy sauce

• 2 tablespoons gochujang (Korean red pepper paste)

• 2 tablespoons honey

• Sesame seeds and green onions for garnish

Instructions:

• Mix soy sauce, gochujang, and honey for glaze.

• Coat wings in glaze, air fry at 380°F for 20-25 minutes.

• Garnish with sesame seeds and chopped green onions.

Servings: 4
Calories: Approximately 340 per serving
Prep Time: 35 minutes

Beef, Pork, and Lamb

Spicy Grilled Steak

Ingredients:
- 1.5 pounds sirloin or ribeye steak

- 2 tablespoons olive oil

- 2 teaspoons smoked paprika

- 1 teaspoon cayenne pepper

- 1 teaspoon garlic powder

- Salt and pepper to taste

Instructions:

- In a bowl, mix olive oil, smoked paprika, cayenne pepper, garlic powder, salt, and pepper to create the marinade.

• Rub the steak generously with the marinade, ensuring it's well coated. Let it marinate for at least 30 minutes.

• Preheat your air fryer to 400°F.

• Place the marinated steak in the air fryer basket, making sure it's a single layer for even cooking.

• Air fry for 10-12 minutes for medium-rare, adjusting time based on your desired doneness.

• Allow the steak to rest for a few minutes before slicing.

Servings: 4
Calories: Approximately 350 per serving
Prep Time: 40 minutes

Beef and Cheese Empanadas

Ingredients:
• 1 pound ground beef

• 1 cup shredded cheddar cheese

• 1 small onion, finely chopped

• 2 cloves garlic, minced

• 1 teaspoon cumin

• 1 teaspoon paprika

• Salt and pepper to taste

• Empanada dough (store-bought or homemade)

Instructions:

• In a pan, cook ground beef until browned. Add onion, garlic, cumin, paprika, salt, and pepper. Cook until onions are softened.

• Roll out empanada dough and cut into circles.

• Spoon a portion of the beef mixture onto each dough circle, top with cheese, fold, and seal the edges.

• Preheat your air fryer to 375°F.

• Place empanadas in the air fryer basket, ensuring they're not touching.

• Air fry for 12-15 minutes until golden brown and crispy.

Servings: 6
Calories: Approximately 280 per serving
Prep Time: 50 minutes

Beef and Broccoli

Ingredients:
• 1.5 pounds beef sirloin, thinly sliced

• 2 cups broccoli florets

• 1/3 cup soy sauce

• 2 tablespoons oyster sauce

• 2 tablespoons brown sugar

• 2 cloves garlic, minced

• 1 teaspoon ginger, grated

• 1 tablespoon cornstarch

• Sesame seeds and green onions for garnish

Instructions:

• In a bowl, mix soy sauce, oyster sauce, brown sugar, garlic, ginger, and cornstarch to create the sauce.

• Marinate the sliced beef in half of the sauce for 15-20 minutes.

• Preheat your air fryer to 375°F.

• Place marinated beef and broccoli in the air fryer basket.

• Air fry for 10-12 minutes, shaking the basket halfway.

• Drizzle with the remaining sauce, garnish with sesame seeds and green onions before serving.

Servings: 4
Calories: Approximately 320 per serving
Prep Time: 35 minutes

Meatballs in Spicy Tomato Sauce

Ingredients:
- 1.5 pounds ground beef

- 1/2 cup breadcrumbs

- 1/4 cup grated Parmesan cheese

- 2 cloves garlic, minced

- 1 teaspoon dried oregano

- 1/2 teaspoon red pepper flakes

- Salt and pepper to taste

- 2 cups tomato sauce

Instructions:

• In a bowl, combine ground beef, breadcrumbs, Parmesan cheese, garlic, oregano, red pepper flakes, salt, and pepper. Form into meatballs.

• Preheat your air fryer to 375°F.

• Place meatballs in the air fryer basket, ensuring space between each.

• Air fry for 15-18 minutes until golden brown and cooked through.

• Heat tomato sauce separately and serve meatballs over the sauce.

Servings: 6
Calories: Approximately 290 per serving
Prep Time: 45 minutes

Taco Pizza

Ingredients:

• 1 pound ground beef

• 1 packet taco seasoning

- 1/2 cup salsa

- 1 cup shredded cheddar cheese

- 1 cup shredded lettuce

- 1 cup diced tomatoes

- 1/4 cup sliced black olives

- 1/4 cup chopped green onions

- 1 pre-made pizza dough

Instructions:

- Preheat your air fryer to 375°F.

- Cook ground beef, drain excess fat, and mix in taco seasoning.

- Roll out pizza dough and place it in the air fryer basket.

• Spread salsa on the dough, add seasoned ground beef, and top with cheese.

• Air fry for 10-12 minutes until crust is golden.

• Remove from the air fryer, and add lettuce, tomatoes, olives, and green onions.

Servings: 4
Calories: Approximately 340 per serving
Prep Time: 55 minutes

Panko-Crusted Boneless Pork Chops

Ingredients:

• 4 boneless pork chops

• 1 cup panko breadcrumbs

• 1/2 cup grated Parmesan cheese

• 1 teaspoon garlic powder

• 1 teaspoon dried thyme

• Salt and pepper to taste

• 2 eggs, beaten

Instructions:

• Preheat your air fryer to 400°F.

• In a shallow dish, mix panko, Parmesan, garlic powder, thyme, salt, and pepper.

• Dip each pork chop into the beaten eggs, then coat with the breadcrumb mixture.

• Place the coated pork chops in the air fryer basket.

• Air fry for 12-15 minutes, flipping halfway, until the coating is golden and the pork is cooked through.

Servings: 4
Calories: Approximately 280 per serving
Prep Time: 25 minutes

Lemon Pork Tenderloin

Ingredients:

• 1.5 pounds pork tenderloin

• Zest and juice of 2 lemons

• 2 tablespoons olive oil

• 3 cloves garlic, minced

• 1 teaspoon dried oregano

• Salt and pepper to taste

Instructions:

• Preheat your air fryer to 375°F.

• In a bowl, mix lemon zest, lemon juice, olive oil, garlic, oregano, salt, and pepper.

• Rub the mixture over the pork tenderloin, ensuring it's evenly coated.

• Place the pork tenderloin in the air fryer basket.

• Air fry for 20-25 minutes, turning once halfway, until the internal temperature reaches 145°F.

Servings: 4
Calories: Approximately 220 per serving
Prep Time: 30 minutes

Barbecued Baby Back Ribs

Ingredients:

• 2 racks baby back ribs

• 1 cup barbecue sauce

• 2 teaspoons smoked paprika

• 1 teaspoon onion powder

• 1 teaspoon garlic powder

• Salt and pepper to taste

Instructions:

• Preheat your air fryer to 375°F.

• Mix barbecue sauce, smoked paprika, onion powder, garlic powder, salt, and pepper in a bowl.

• Brush the ribs with the barbecue mixture, ensuring they are well coated.

• Place the ribs in the air fryer basket.

• Air fry for 25-30 minutes, brushing with additional sauce halfway, until the ribs are tender.

Servings: 4
Calories: Approximately 450 per serving
Prep Time: 40 minutes

Pork Teriyaki

Ingredients:

- 1.5 pounds pork loin, thinly sliced

- 1/2 cup soy sauce

- 1/4 cup mirin

- 2 tablespoons brown sugar

- 2 cloves garlic, minced

- 1 teaspoon grated ginger

- Sesame seeds and green onions for garnish

Instructions:

- In a bowl, mix soy sauce, mirin, brown sugar, garlic, and ginger to create the teriyaki sauce.

- Marinate the sliced pork in the sauce for at least 30 minutes.

- Preheat your air fryer to 400°F.

- Place marinated pork in the air fryer basket, ensuring it's a single layer.

• Air fry for 10-12 minutes, shaking the basket halfway.

• Garnish with sesame seeds and green onions before serving.

Servings: 4
Calories: Approximately 320 per serving
Prep Time: 45 minutes

Greek Lamb Burgers

Ingredients:
• 1 pound ground lamb

• 1/2 cup feta cheese, crumbled

• 1/4 cup red onion, finely chopped

• 1 teaspoon dried oregano

• 1 teaspoon garlic powder

• Salt and pepper to taste

• Tzatziki sauce for serving

Instructions:

• Preheat your air fryer to 375°F.

• In a bowl, mix ground lamb, feta, red onion, oregano, garlic powder, salt, and pepper.

• Form the mixture into burger patties.

• Place the lamb burgers in the air fryer basket.

• Air fry for 12-15 minutes, flipping once, until the burgers are cooked to your liking.

• Serve with tzatziki sauce.

Servings: 4
Calories: Approximately 340 per serving
Prep Time: 30 minutes

Dessert

Marble Cheesecake

Ingredients:
• 2 cups cream cheese, softened

• 1 cup granulated sugar

• 3 large eggs

• 1 teaspoon vanilla extract

• 1/4 cup all-purpose flour

• 1/4 cup cocoa powder

• Chocolate syrup for drizzling

Instructions:

• Preheat your air fryer to 320°F.

• In a bowl, beat cream cheese and sugar until smooth.

• Add eggs one at a time, beating well after each addition.

• Stir in vanilla extract.

• Divide the batter in half. Mix flour into one half and cocoa powder into the other.

• Layer the batters in a greased springform pan.

• Use a skewer to create a marble pattern.

• Air fry for 35-40 minutes, until the center is set.

• Drizzle with chocolate syrup before serving.

Servings: 8
Calories: Approximately 350 per serving
Prep Time: 20 minutes

Chocolate Peanut Butter Bread Pudding

Ingredients:
• 4 cups bread cubes

- 1/2 cup chocolate chips

- 1/2 cup peanut butter

- 2 cups milk

- 3 large eggs

- 1/2 cup granulated sugar

- 1 teaspoon vanilla extract

Instructions:

- Preheat your air fryer to 350°F.

- In a bowl, combine bread cubes and chocolate chips.

- In a separate bowl, whisk together peanut butter, milk, eggs, sugar, and vanilla extract.

- Pour the wet mixture over the bread cubes and toss to coat.

• Transfer to a greased baking dish.

• Air fry for 25-30 minutes, until the pudding is set.

Servings: 6
Calories: Approximately 400 per serving
Prep Time: 15 minutes

Pineapple Cream Cheese Wontons

Ingredients:
• 1 cup cream cheese, softened

• 1 cup crushed pineapple, drained

• 1/4 cup powdered sugar

• Wonton wrappers

Instructions:

• Preheat your air fryer to 375°F.

• In a bowl, mix cream cheese, crushed pineapple, and powdered sugar.

• Place a spoonful of the mixture in the center of each wonton wrapper.

• Wet the edges and fold into triangles, sealing the edges.

• Air fry for 8-10 minutes, until golden and crispy.

Servings: 4
Calories: Approximately 250 per serving
Prep Time: 20 minutes

Honey-Roasted Pears with Ricotta

Ingredients:
• 4 ripe pears, halved and cored

• 2 tablespoons honey

• 1/2 cup ricotta cheese

• Chopped pistachios for garnish

Instructions:

- Preheat your air fryer to 375°F.

- Brush pear halves with honey.

- Air fry for 15-18 minutes, until pears are tender.

- Fill each pear half with a spoonful of ricotta.

- Garnish with chopped pistachios before serving.

Servings: 4
Calories: Approximately 180 per serving
Prep Time: 15 minutes

Gooey Lemon Bars

Ingredients:
- 1 cup all-purpose flour

- 1/2 cup unsalted butter, softened

- 1/4 cup powdered sugar

- 2 large eggs

- 1 cup granulated sugar

- 2 tablespoons all-purpose flour

- 1/2 teaspoon baking powder

- Zest and juice of 2 lemons

- Powdered sugar for dusting

Instructions:
- Preheat your air fryer to 325°F.

- In a bowl, mix flour, butter, and powdered sugar to make the crust.

- Press the crust into a greased baking dish.

- In another bowl, beat eggs, granulated sugar, flour, baking powder, lemon zest, and lemon juice.

- Pour the lemon mixture over the crust.

• Air fry for 20-25 minutes, until the edges are golden.

• Cool before dusting with powdered sugar.

Servings: 9
Calories: Approximately 220 per serving
Prep Time: 25 minutes

Baked Apples

Ingredients:
• 4 large apples, cored

• 1/4 cup brown sugar

• 1 teaspoon cinnamon

• 2 tablespoons unsalted butter

• 1/4 cup chopped nuts (optional)

Instructions:

• Preheat your air fryer to 375°F.

• In a bowl, mix brown sugar and cinnamon.

• Fill each cored apple with the sugar-cinnamon mixture.

• Place a small piece of butter on top of each filled apple.

• Air fry for 15-20 minutes, until apples are tender.

• Sprinkle with chopped nuts if desired.

Servings: 4
Calories: Approximately 180 per serving
Prep Time: 10 minutes

Apple-Cinnamon Hand Pies

Ingredients:
• 2 refrigerated pie crusts

• 2 cups diced apples

• 1/4 cup granulated sugar

- 1 teaspoon cinnamon

- 1 tablespoon lemon juice

- 1 tablespoon cornstarch

- 1 egg (for egg wash)

Instructions:
- Preheat your air fryer to 375°F.

- In a bowl, mix diced apples, sugar, cinnamon, lemon juice, and cornstarch.

- Roll out the pie crusts and cut into circles.

- Spoon apple mixture onto half of each circle.

- Fold the other half over, sealing the edges with a fork.

- Brush each hand pie with beaten egg.

- Air fry for 12-15 minutes, until golden.

Servings: 8

Calories: Approximately 220 per serving
Prep Time: 20 minutes

Easy Cherry Pie

Ingredients:
• 2 refrigerated pie crusts

• 2 cans cherry pie filling

• 1/2 cup granulated sugar

• 1 tablespoon cornstarch

• 1 egg (for egg wash)

Instructions:

• Preheat your air fryer to 375°F.

• In a bowl, mix cherry pie filling, sugar, and cornstarch.

• Roll out the pie crusts and place one in the bottom of your air fryer basket.

- Pour the cherry mixture over the crust.

- Cover with the second pie crust and seal the edges.

- Brush the top crust with beaten egg.

- Air fry for 20-25 minutes, until the crust is golden.

Servings: 8
Calories: Approximately 280 per serving
Prep Time: 15 minutes

Strawberry-Rhubarb Crumble

Ingredients:
- 3 cups sliced rhubarb

- 2 cups sliced strawberries

- 1/2 cup granulated sugar

- 1/2 cup brown sugar

- 1 cup old-fashioned oats

- 1/2 cup all-purpose flour

- 1/2 cup unsalted butter, melted

Instructions:

- Preheat your air fryer to 375°F.

- In a bowl, mix rhubarb, strawberries, granulated sugar, and brown sugar.

- In a separate bowl, combine oats, flour, and melted butter to make the crumble topping.

- Place the fruit mixture in a baking dish and top with the crumble.

- Air fry for 15-20 minutes, until the top is crisp.

Servings: 6
Calories: Approximately 300 per serving
Prep Time: 15 minutes

**Big Chocolate Chip Cookie
Ingredients:**

- 1 cup all-purpose flour

- 1/2 teaspoon baking soda

- 1/4 teaspoon salt

- 1/2 cup unsalted butter, softened

- 1/3 cup granulated sugar

- 1/2 cup brown sugar

- 1 large egg

- 1 teaspoon vanilla extract

- 1 cup chocolate chips

Instructions:

- Preheat your air fryer to 325°F.

- In a bowl, whisk together flour, baking soda, and salt.

• In another bowl, cream together butter, granulated sugar, and brown sugar until smooth.

• Beat in the egg and vanilla extract.

• Gradually add the dry ingredients and mix until combined.

• Fold in chocolate chips.

• Form the dough into a large cookie in the air fryer basket.

• Air fry for 12-15 minutes, until the edges are golden.

Servings: 4
Calories: Approximately 400 per serving
Prep Time: 20 minutes

Bonus Ninja Air Fryer 1-Week Meal Plan and Shopping List

Creating a balanced and flavorful meal plan with your Ninja® Air Fryer can be a delightful journey into the world of delicious, healthy cooking. Here's a 1-week meal plan that showcases the versatility of your air fryer, covering breakfast, lunch, dinner, and even some snacks.

Day 1

Breakfast: *Avocado and Egg Toast*

• Ingredients: Sliced bread, avocado, eggs.

• Instructions: Top bread with mashed avocado and a fried egg, air fry until the bread is crispy.

Lunch: *Caprese Stuffed Chicken Breast*

• Ingredients: Chicken breast, mozzarella cheese, tomato, basil.

• Instructions: Stuff chicken breast with mozzarella, tomato, and basil, air fry until golden.

Dinner: *Crispy Salmon with Roasted Vegetables*

• Ingredients: Salmon fillets, mixed vegetables, olive oil.

• Instructions: Season salmon and vegetables, air fry until the salmon is crispy and the vegetables are tender.

Day 2
Breakfast: *Blueberry Pancake Bites*

• Ingredients: Pancake batter, fresh blueberries.

• Instructions: Pour batter into small molds, add blueberries, air fry until golden.

Lunch: *Turkey and Veggie Quesadillas*

• Ingredients: Turkey slices, mixed vegetables, cheese, tortillas.

• Instructions: Assemble quesadillas, air fry until the cheese is melted and tortillas are crispy.

Dinner: *Teriyaki Chicken Skewers with Fried Rice*

• Ingredients: Chicken skewers, teriyaki sauce, cooked rice, mixed vegetables.

• Instructions: Coat chicken in teriyaki sauce, air fry skewers, serve with fried rice.

Day 3
Breakfast: *Banana Walnut Muffins*

• Ingredients: Banana muffin batter, chopped walnuts.

• Instructions: Fill muffin cups, sprinkle with walnuts, air fry until muffins are cooked through.

Lunch: *Chicken Caesar Salad Wraps*

• Ingredients: Grilled chicken, lettuce, Caesar dressing, tortillas.

• Instructions: Fill tortillas with chicken, lettuce, and dressing, air fry until warm.

Dinner: *Vegetarian Egg Rolls with Sweet and Sour Sauce*

• Ingredients: Egg roll wrappers, mixed vegetables, sweet and sour sauce.

• Instructions: Fill wrappers, air fry until golden, serve with sauce.

Day 4
Breakfast: *Spinach and Feta Omelette*

• Ingredients: Eggs, fresh spinach, feta cheese.

• Instructions: Whisk eggs, add spinach and feta, air fry until the omelette is set.

Lunch: *BLT Sandwiches*

• Ingredients: Bacon, lettuce, tomato, bread.

• Instructions: Cook bacon, assemble sandwiches, air fry for a crispy finish.

Dinner: *Crispy Air-Fried Shrimp Tacos*

• Ingredients: Shrimp, taco shells, cabbage, salsa.

• Instructions: Season shrimp, air fry until crispy, assemble tacos.

Day 5
Breakfast: *Cinnamon Sugar Donuts*

• Ingredients: Biscuit dough, cinnamon sugar.

• Instructions: Cut biscuit dough into rounds, air fry, coat in cinnamon sugar.

Lunch: *Greek Chicken Gyros*

• Ingredients: Chicken strips, pita bread, cucumber, tzatziki sauce.

• Instructions: Air fry chicken, assemble gyros with veggies and sauce.

Dinner: *Beef and Broccoli Stir Fry*

• Ingredients: Beef strips, broccoli, soy sauce, rice.

• Instructions: Stir fry beef and broccoli, air fry for extra crispiness.

Day 6
Breakfast: *Breakfast Pizza*

• Ingredients: Pizza dough, eggs, bacon, cheese.

• Instructions: Top dough with eggs, bacon, and cheese, air fry until the crust is golden.

Lunch: *Southwest Chicken Egg Rolls*

• Ingredients: Chicken, black beans, corn, egg roll wrappers.

• Instructions: Fill wrappers, air fry until crispy, serve with salsa.

Dinner: *Salmon on a Bed of Fennel and Carrot*

• Ingredients: Salmon fillets, fennel, carrots, lemon.

• Instructions: Season salmon and vegetables, air fry until the salmon is cooked through.

Day 7
Breakfast: *Fruit Parfait*

• Ingredients: Greek yogurt, granola, mixed fruits.

• Instructions: Layer yogurt, granola, and fruits in jars, air fry for a warm parfait.

Lunch: *Vegetarian Stuffed Bell Peppers*

• Ingredients: Bell peppers, quinoa, black beans, cheese.

• Instructions: Stuff peppers, air fry until cheese is melted.

Dinner: *Barbecue Chicken Drumsticks with Potato Wedges*

• Ingredients: Chicken drumsticks, barbecue sauce, potatoes.

• Instructions: Coat drumsticks in barbecue sauce, air fry until crispy, serve with wedges.

This meal plan offers a variety of flavors and cuisines, showcasing the Ninja® Air Fryer's versatility. Adjust portions based on your dietary needs and enjoy exploring the world of air-fried delights!

Shopping List

Embarking on a culinary adventure with your Ninja® Air Fryer requires a well-curated shopping list to ensure you have all the ingredients at your fingertips. Let's delve into the art of crafting a versatile and practical shopping list, drawing inspiration from a seasoned chef's perspective.

Fresh Produce

• **Avocado**: Creamy and nutritious, perfect for morning toasts or salads.

• **Eggs**: A kitchen staple for numerous air-fried recipes, from breakfast omelets to dinner frittatas.

• **Tomatoes**: Ideal for caprese-stuffed chicken or as a base for various sauces.

• **Basil**: A fragrant herb that adds a burst of flavor to dishes like caprese-stuffed chicken.

• **Mixed Vegetables**: Versatile for salads, stir-fries, and air-fried sides.

Fruits

• **Blueberries**: A delightful addition to breakfast pancake bites and desserts.

• **Bananas**: Essential for muffins or as a quick, nutritious snack.

- **Strawberries**: Perfect for desserts or a refreshing addition to salads.

- **Lemon**: Adds a zesty kick to seafood dishes like lemony salmon fillets.

Dairy

- **Mozzarella Cheese**: Melts beautifully for stuffed chicken or pizza.

- **Cheddar Cheese**: Essential for savory dishes like loaded breakfast burritos.

- **Feta Cheese**: Elevates the flavor of omelets and salads.

- **Greek Yogurt**: A versatile ingredient for breakfast parfaits or as a base for various sauces.

Breads and Grains

- **Sliced Bread**: An essential for breakfast toasts or making sandwiches.

• **Tortillas**: Versatile for wraps, quesadillas, and burritos.

• **Pancake Batter**: Simplifies the preparation of pancake bites and other breakfast treats.

• **Pizza Dough**: For crafting quick and easy air-fried pizzas or breakfast pizza.

Proteins

• **Chicken Breast**: Lean and versatile, suitable for a variety of air-fried dishes.

• **Salmon Fillets**: Rich in omega-3 fatty acids, perfect for air-fried seafood delights.

• **Ground Turkey**: Ideal for preparing flavorful and lean air-fried dishes.

• **Shrimp**: Quick-cooking and versatile, great for tacos or crispy air-fried shrimp.

Pantry Staples

• **Olive Oil**: A kitchen essential for seasoning and sautéing.

• **Teriyaki Sauce**: Adds a sweet and savory touch to various dishes.

• **Soy Sauce**: A versatile ingredient for stir-fries and marinades.

• **Spices and Herbs**: Customize your seasoning blend based on personal preferences.

Frozen Items

• **Mixed Vegetables**: Convenient for quick stir-fries or as side dishes.

• **Pizza Rolls or Egg Rolls**: Perfect for a hassle-free snack or appetizer.

• **Chicken Drumsticks**: A freezer staple for an easy dinner with barbecue sauce.

Miscellaneous

• **Biscuit Dough**: Simplifies the preparation of cinnamon sugar donuts or other sweet treats.

• **Quinoa**: A nutritious grain for stuffed bell peppers or salads.

• **Barbecue Sauce**: Elevates the flavor of barbecue chicken drumsticks.

• **Potatoes**: Versatile for making wedges or pairing with various dishes.

Crafting a thoughtful shopping list ensures you're well-prepared to explore the vast possibilities your Ninja® Air Fryer offers. It's not just a list; it's a gateway to culinary creativity and a well-stocked kitchen ready for delightful air-fried adventures. Happy cooking!

Measurement Conversions

Understanding measurement conversions is crucial for precise and successful cooking. Here's a quick reference guide to common measurement conversions:

Volume Conversions

1. Teaspoon (tsp):

• 1 teaspoon = 5 milliliters (ml)

2. Tablespoon (tbsp):

• 1 tablespoon = 15 milliliters (ml)

• 3 teaspoons = 1 tablespoon

3. Fluid Ounce (fl oz):

• 1 fluid ounce = 30 milliliters (ml)

• 2 tablespoons = 1 fluid ounce

4. Cup (c):

• 1 cup = 240 milliliters (ml)

• 8 fluid ounces = 1 cup

5. Pint (pt):

• 1 pint = 480 milliliters (ml)

• 2 cups = 1 pint

6. Quart (qt):

• 1 quart = 960 milliliters (ml)

• 4 cups = 1 quart

7. Gallon (gal):

• 1 gallon = 3,840 milliliters (ml)

• 4 quarts = 1 gallon

Weight Conversions

1. Ounce (oz):

• 1 ounce = 28.35 grams (g)

• 16 ounces = 1 pound

2. Pound (lb):

- 1 pound = 453.59 grams (g)

- 16 ounces = 1 pound

Temperature Conversions

1. Celsius to Fahrenheit:

- °F = (°C × 9/5) + 32

2. Fahrenheit to Celsius:

- °C = (°F − 32) × 5/9

Length Conversions

1. Inch (in):

- 1 inch = 2.54 centimeters (cm)

2. Foot (ft):

- 1 foot = 30.48 centimeters (cm)

- 12 inches = 1 foot

3. Meter (m):

- 1 meter = 39.37 inches

- 1 meter = 3.28 feet

These conversions should help you navigate various recipes and ensure your culinary creations turn out just right. Happy cooking!

Printed in Great Britain
by Amazon